THE GREEDY GAME
A KID'S INTRO TO MICROTRANSACTIONS

L FAIRLIGHT

I recently got my first phone.
My favourite thing about it has been
all the games I can play.

But there's something
that's been bothering me...

There's this one
game a lot
of my friends
have been
playing that I
downloaded.

It's a free game,
so almost everyone
is playing it.

You play an adventurer in a big world,
fighting monsters and getting treasure.

It was fun for a while, but there's a problem...

If you want to get stronger,
you need to get new stuff from loot boxes.

They gave me the
first few for free,
but then if you want
more, you have
to buy them with
real money.

All my friends were way stronger than me and it felt almost impossible to play without spending money.

"You're not even helping! You need some better armour and weapons!"

We have parental controls on my phone so I can't accidentally spend money, so I asked my mum if I could use my pocket money to buy some loot boxes to keep up with my friends.

But she just said "NO WAY!"

I asked my classmates at school what to do, but they all had different opinions.

"Just stop playing that game, it sounds stupid anyway."

"Hack it and spend the money anyway. Maybe you're just not cool enough to play the game."

"I've been thinking of quitting too. I already spent all my pocket money on loot boxes and now I can't afford the skateboard I was saving up for."

"Just play it for free and don't buy the boxes. It takes a long time to level up, but if you're patient it's okay."

I didn't like how the game made me feel, and I didn't like the peer pressure to spend my pocket money so I deleted the game and downloaded another one...

This one was a HUGE game I could even play on the computer!

This game had it's own currency:

PUPPYBUX

You could buy PUPPYBUX with real dollars, but you could also earn PUPPYBUX in the game to buy more stuff.

The game said you could also turn your PUPPYBUX back into real dollars if you wanted your money back again.

It sounded really good...

You could even make your own games that other kids could buy with PUPPYBUX, so you could make money in the game even though you're just a kid!

I spent ages programming my own game!

I was so excited to start
earning PUPPYBUX!

But there was a problem...
Nobody was seeing my game!

DOWNLOADS: 0

If I wanted people to buy it, I'd have to advertise!

I could pay for ads with PUPPYBUX, but I didn't have enough.

My mum was really strict about not putting money into a game, but this was a BUSINESS!

I was so confident if people just saw my game they'd buy it.

Then I'd be a

PUPPILLIONAIRE!

One of my classmates had a solution,
but it made me a bit uneasy...

"I could pay for the ads for you,
but you'd owe me BIG TIME!"

But my best friend had some better advice.

"Maybe you just need to talk to
your mum about how important
this is for you."

"You really think
she'll listen?"

"I'm sure she will."

So I explained to my mum how much work I'd put into this game and how I NEEDED to have some PUPPYBUX to get my game in front of other kids.

This wasn't just about one game, this was the beginning of my future career as a game designer!

But she still had some concerns...

"Aren't you still just taking money off other kids?

We need to have a look into this!"

That was when things got really serious...

IS PUPPYBUX A SCAM? 🔍

Mum looked up the game on her phone and she found out a lot of stuff...

I realized I didn't really understand how it worked at all...

First of all, you could buy PUPPYBUX for as little as $5 real dollars... but if you wanted to convert PUPPYBUX back into real money you had to have a minimum of $1000 PUPPYBUX!

EASY

HARD

In other words, it was easy to buy PUPPYBUX but really hard to turn PUPPYBUX back into real money.

Even if I was to buy ads, I would need to make so many sales of my game that it would be really hard to ever make enough PUPPYBUX to get any real money back.

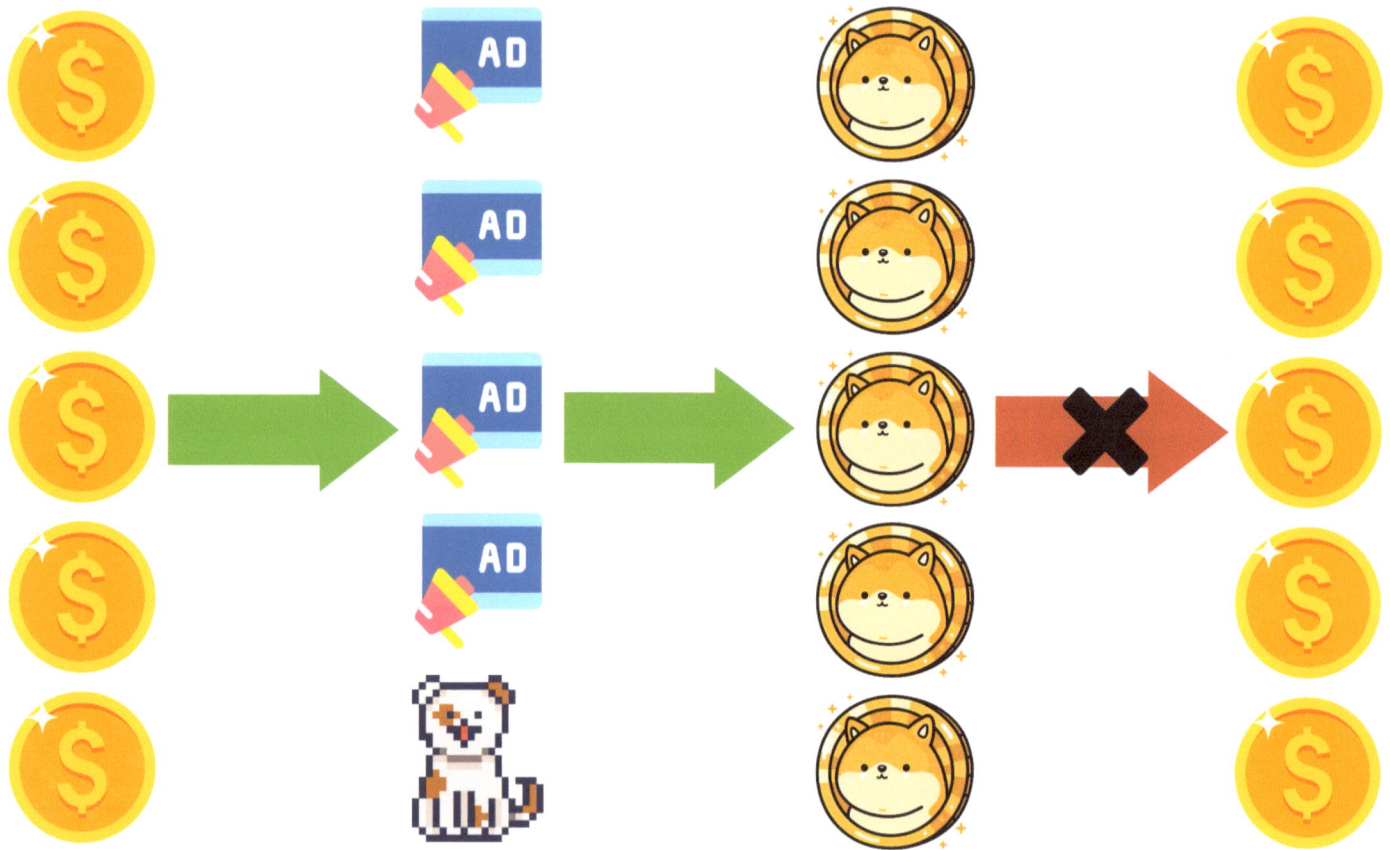

Most kids never earned anything,
but they would spend a lot on ads.

I was heartbroken.

I wanted to make fun games, but everything I'd played just seemed to be making a game out of getting money out of me.

Mum saw how sad I was
but she told me not to give up.

She told me the time I spent making that game
wasn't wasted because I still learned a lot of
skills.

She also told me that one of my relatives,
Cousin Jerry, was a game designer.

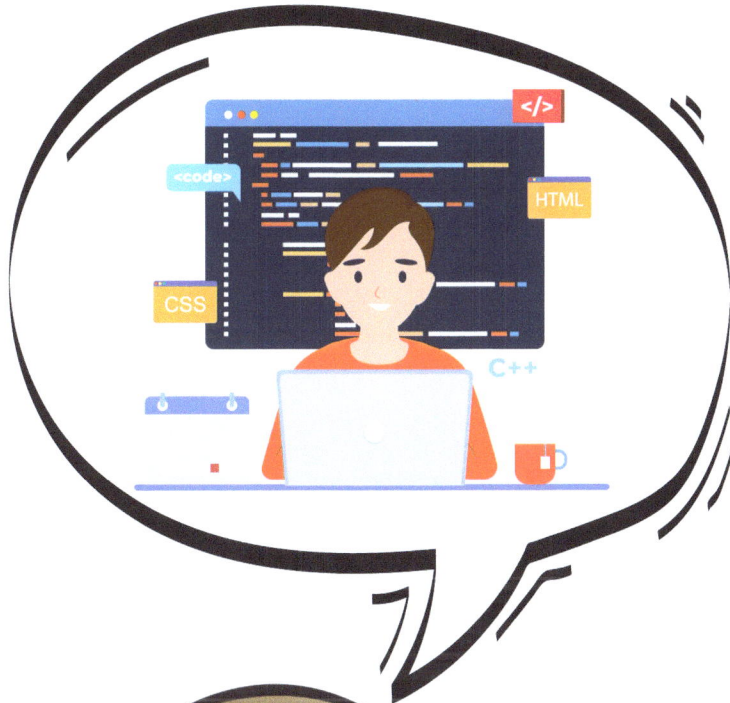

He could talk to me about how to design games well without scamming anyone or getting scammed myself!

Jerry said he was really sorry that this was my first experience with games.

He explained to me that the games industry was a really fun place to work, but there were always lots of challenges.

There are a lot of different ways games are designed, and its good to know the difference between them.

Designing games takes a lot of time and talent - as I'd discovered from all that time I put into making my own game!

So the game designers have to figure out how they will get paid for their work.

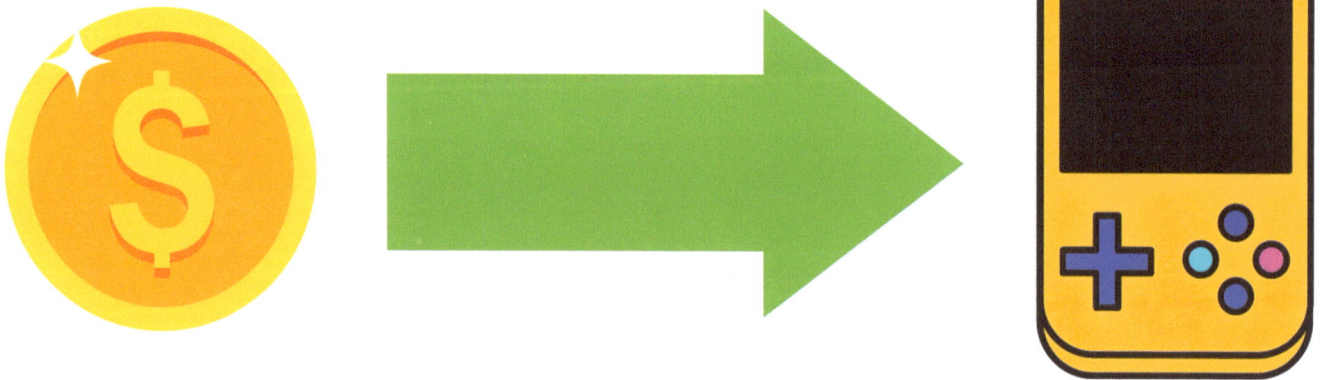

Some games are paid for with real money upfront.

If a game is free to download, it usually will find another way to make money.

A lot of people don't mind if you just buy things like accessories and outfits - but sometimes it can become impossible to keep playing without spending money.

They might start you off for free, but if you have to spend real money to keep playing the game, it is

PAY TO PLAY

When a game starts selling items that impact gameplay, then it becomes

PAY TO WIN

This might look like paying for weapons or outfits that give you extra speed or power.

If you need to buy things to win, the game has been designed to be unbalanced.

The real game is trying to see how much money it can make you spend.

All these little purchases are called

MICRO-TRANSACTIONS

It can be really easy to spend a dollar here and there on a game...

EASY

But all those dollars add up and you can find out you've spent more than you intended!

Loot boxes are effective ways to get people to spend a lot of money, because you're not buying an item - you're buying a CHANCE to get an item.

So people often end up buying a lot of them for better chances to get the items they want - but they can spend a lot.

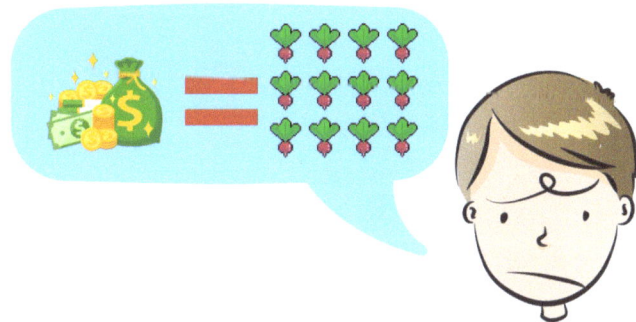

Another thing people often spend microtransactions on are skins, accessories, and emotes, to make their characters look more custom and unique.

Sometimes kids get cyberbullied and pressured into paying for these cosmetic upgrades.

♥💔1

"EW, DEFAULT!"

It can feel like they're worth more than they are, especially if there's a marketplace you can sell them on, but you have to consider how hard it is to get your money back.

HARD

Remember: it's a purchase, NOT an investment.

Jerry also said that there's a lot of other ways that game designers can make money without relying on these techniques.

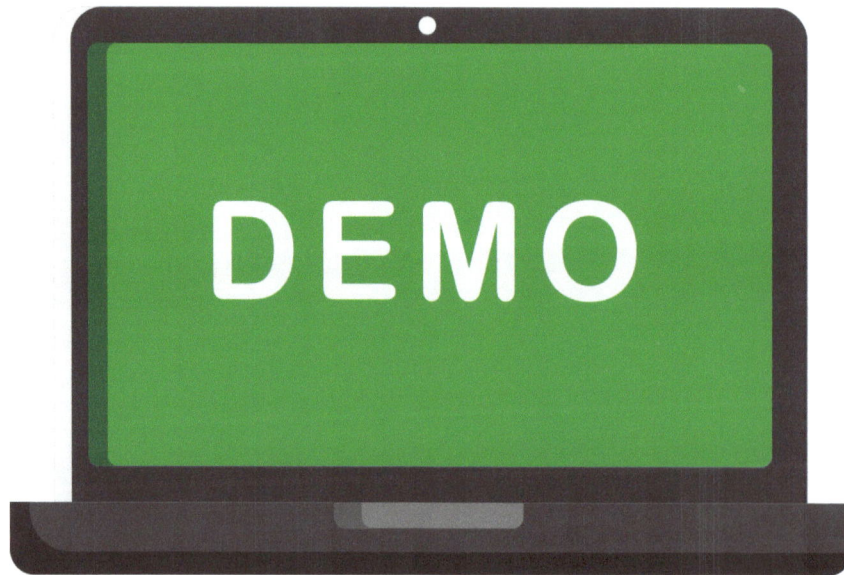

DEMO

While a lot of games are paid for upfront, some games will allow you to play a free demo of the game so you can see if you like it - then you can buy the full game when the demo is over if you want it.

But he said demos are different from subscription game trials, which are when they give you a period of time for free but then will start charging you a subscription fee to play.

7 DAYS FREE TRIAL

$10 PER WEEK PRO VERSION

He said if they ask you to enter any details like your credit card number to play, it's a red flag and to go ask for help from an adult - even if it says it's free to play.

Games should not need any of your personal details to function.

Other games will allow you to play the game for free and make money off ads. Sometimes you can pay money to upgrade to an ad-free version of the game.

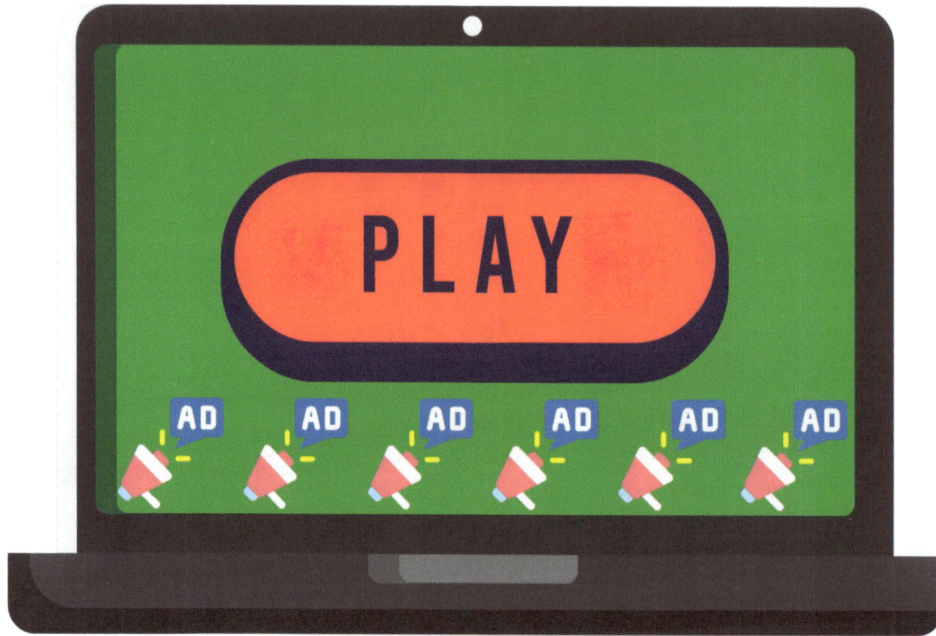

PLAY

AD AD AD AD AD AD

But Jerry also warned me not all ads are appropriate for children, so to be careful and tell my mum if anything popped up that I didn't feel was right!

Other games will give you the base game but then there will be new levels, areas or expansions that you can buy as well.

This is another legitimate way that game designers make money off their hard work.

FREE!

BUY NOW

BUY NOW

Jerry told me to keep designing!

He'll play any game I make and give me feedback.

He reminded me to check games for
"social proof" and hidden problems,
and to think twice when games ask for extra money.

GAME REVIEW

APP

5 MILLION DOWNLOADS
★★★★★
"GREAT APP,
PERFECT FOR KIDS"

APP

5000 DOWNLOADS
★★
"HATE THIS APP, CHARGED MY
ACCOUNT AND NO REFUND"

Jerry set me up on some kid-friendly game designing websites that had a good reputation, so I'll be practicing making games there.

I've learned a lot about being careful about choosing which games I play - and not letting them play me instead!

I've also learned that I need to go to my mum for help.

Even if she doesn't have the answers, she often knows someone else who we can go and talk to until we can figure the problem out!

SET YOUR BOUNDARIES

What rules do you have about downloading new games or apps?

How can you work together to check which games are suitable?

Are you okay with spending money on games?

What is your budget?

Would you prefer to buy standalone games at full price which don't have ads or microtransactions?

Do you understand the terms and conditions of the game or website properly?

What do you do if you feel uncomfortable about something?
Are you comfortable going to your parents, even if you think you might have made a mistake?

NOTE FROM THE AUTHOR

Kia Ora from sunny New Zealand!

One of my first jobs out of school was managing a game shop. I absolutely love the gaming industry and I think it can be a wonderful place for people to have fun, be creative and make friends.

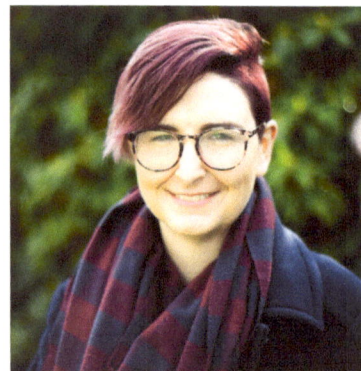

I've watched it change over the last couple of decades, and since having kids I've realized a lot of parents aren't well-equipped to teach their kids about the pitfalls they can come across, because unless they're in it themselves, how do they know? We don't all have the benefit of a Cousin Jerry.

I've also noticed a lot of the educational content out there is aimed at older kids and teenagers, but kids are getting devices a lot younger than that! I designed these books to give parents and teachers resources to go through with their kids and help them understand and recognize some of the dangers so they can navigate the digital world with confidence - and know when to ask for help.

Thank you for purchasing this book. I'd LOVE it if you could also recommend this book to your local school and library as well - I'd like to keep making more resources for kids to learn about the world - but just like with game designers, developing and publishing books costs money!

I've developed some extra resources and printable activities and which I have available on my website for free!
https://laurawolfbookclub.wordpress.com/cyber-kids/

CHECK OUT THE REST OF THE SERIES

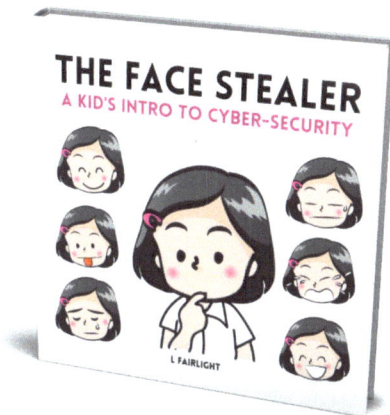

THE FACE STEALER
A KID'S INTRO TO CYBER-SECURITY

L FAIRLIGHT

THE FAKE FACT
A KID'S INTRO TO MISINFORMATION

L FAIRLIGHT

THE TINY TRICK
A KID'S INTRO TO CYBER SECURITY

THINKING BEFORE YOU CLICK

APP PERMISSIONS

L FAIRLIGHT

No one ever expects the face stealer to steal their face - until it happens to them...

Kids are getting exposure to the internet - the good and the bad - younger and younger. Even if your kids don't get access to phones and social media apps, they may be exposed to them at friends houses. Conversations need to be had around what can potentially happen if you let people share you photos and information before they are put into a tricky situation.

Get The Face Stealer here:

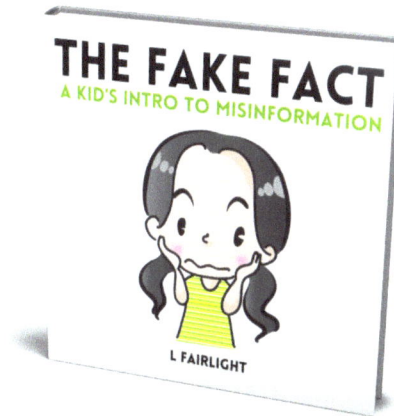

You'd never expect to find out something you believe isn't true... especially when you heard it from your mum!

Follow this little girl's journey as she learns how information travels and can get distorted by either accident or design.

A fantastic educational resource for parents and teachers to help children understand sources, bias and misinformation.

Get The Fake Fact here:

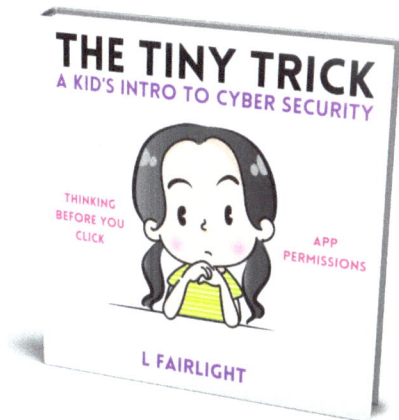

Think before you click agree!

This story of a little girl with her first phone is a great conversation starter to get your kids thinking about what they are agreeing to when they download apps, and what permissions they are allowing in the fine print.

Get The Tiny Trick here:

laurawolfbookclub.wordpress.com/cyber-kids/

ALSO BY L FAIRLIGHT

AGATHA'S FOREST
A KID'S INTRO TO NAMING EMOTIONS
L FAIRLIGHT